NON OF THESE THINGS!:

GOD has Given YOU Divine Health

BY

REV CHRIS

TABLE OF CONTENTS

INTRODUCTION

Is Heavenly Recuperating (Otherworldly Mending, Confidence Mending) for You Today? Indeed!

Does God actually recuperate? Is heavenly mending for now, or only for when Jesus strolled the earth? Could we at any point hope to see extraordinary healing s nowadays in our cutting edge, super advanced world? Indeed! Divine recuperating gave me my 4 youngsters. For the initial six years of our marriage, my better half Mickey experienced a restorative analyzed fruitlessness condition. We yearned for youngsters. I review her approaching home sobbing from a child shower where she had been the main lady present who was not a mother. Solidly accepting that Jesus mends today, we had asked simperingly, and we frequently got petition from others for the recuperating of this barrenness. Then one day a woman in our congregation said that the Master had addressed her around midnight to tell this to my significant other: "Your fruitless days are finished!"

Mickey put "feet to her confidence" by purchasing a roomful of nursery furniture, and we would go into that room frequently and petition God for the child that we were confiding in the Ruler to give us one day to rest in that den.

Indeed, somewhat more than a year after the Ruler had addressed Mickey "Your desolate days are finished!" she conveyed our firstborn child, Brian (we actually consider him our "supernatural occurrence child"). The Master's mending was finished to such an extent that in resulting years Mickey bore us three additional youngsters. So to the people who inquire, "Is heavenly recuperating for now?" I recount my 4 now-grown-up kids as living models. Jehovah-Rapha — The Ruler Our Healer!

My craving in this Book of scriptures study is to show from the book of scriptures' heavenly recuperating Sacred texts that God is both capable and able to mend the debilitated, the sick, the decrepit. My family has actually encountered this gift of God's recuperating power. So have a huge number of others. Large numbers of books have been composed on what is differently called confidence mending, profound recuperating, divine mending, supplication for the debilitated, mending service, and other comparable articulations. What's more, real recuperating declarations proliferate of God's extraordinary ability to make debilitated and sick bodies well. Individuals need and need to understand what God in His Book of scriptures says regarding disorder and recuperating — that is, what heavenly mending implies in Sacred text — and how we can get to and actuate God's healing power.

The establishment for the subject of heavenly healing lies not such a great amount as far as men can tell — as brilliant as that might be — however in the Sacred writings, the Expression of God. So we should go now to the Holy book to see its disclosure of this extraordinary reality of profound recuperating. (Illustrative note: the expressions "otherworldly mending," "divine recuperating," and "confidence recuperating" are basically utilized conversely in this book of scriptures study.)

• Debilitated adherents don't have to stay wiped out!

James 5:14 Is any of you debilitated? He ought to call the elderly folks of the congregation to implore over him... James was keeping in touch with Christian devotees (2:1). He inquired as to whether any of them were wiped out. It is "guaranteed" of life in our fallen condition that our bodies once in a while watch out for disorder, and in the long run they pass on. Notwithstanding, as the refrain straightforwardly underneath brings up, it is likewise "guaranteed" for the devotee that God is Jehovah-Rapha, "the Ruler who recuperates you."

Mass migration 15:26 [God] said, "Assuming you listen cautiously to the voice of the Master your God and make the right decision in his eyes, on the off chance that you focus on his orders and keep every one of his announcements, I won't welcome on you any of the sicknesses I welcomed on the Egyptians, for I'm the Ruler, who mends you."

God recognized Himself to Israel in various names and ways. Here He uncovered Himself to His kin as "Jehovah-Rapha" — "the Master who mends you."

Mending isn't simply something that God "does." No, more than that, recuperating is essential for God's actual nature — "I'm the Master who recuperates you." God was, is, and will keep on being a Healer. Recall generally that you serve a recuperating God who has proclaimed that His plan towards you is "not [to] welcome on you any illnesses ... [but to be] the Ruler who heals you."
• God is FOR us, not against us, in that frame of mind of healing. God's heart towards His kin is well-being and recuperating. Obviously, for instance, the accompanying Sacred writing stanzas on mending:
Departure 23:25-26 Love the Ruler your God, and his approval will be on your food and water. I will remove disorder from among you, and none will prematurely deliver or be fruitless in your property. I will give you a full life expectancy.

Deuteronomy 7:11-12, 15 Hence, take care to follow the orders, announcements and regulations I give you today. On the off chance that you focus on these regulations and are mindful so as to follow them, then the Ruler your

God will keep his pledge of affection with you, as he committed to your forefathers.... [15] The Master will keep you liberated from each illness. He won't cause for you the horrendous illnesses you knew in Egypt, however he will incur them for all who can't stand you.

Acts 10:38 ...how God blessed Jesus of Nazareth with the Essence of God and power, and how he went around accomplishing something useful and mending all who were under the force of Satan, since God was with him.

• God's profound mending power reaches out to Every one of our illnesses and ailments.

Psalms. 103:2-3 Applause the Master, O my spirit, and fail to remember not every one of his advantages — who excuses every one of your wrongdoings and heals every one of your infections.

The best of the Ruler's "benefits" is that He excuses every one of our wrongdoings! Yet, the Psalmist here charges us not to forget one more of the Ruler's advantages — that is, He "recuperates every one of our infections."

Every one of our infections! None are excessively hard for Him. God recuperates them all. No sicknesses are rejected from this extraordinary "benefit." Anything infection you or a friend or family member might have, it falls under God's guarantee to "mend every one of your illnesses."

• Jesus kicked the bucket for both our transgressions and our disorders.

Isaiah 53:5 However he was penetrated for our offenses, he was squashed for our wrongdoings; the discipline that brought us harmony had arrived, and by his injuries we are recuperated.

1 Peter 2:24 He, when all is said and done, bore our wrongdoings in his body on the tree, with the goal that we could pass on to sins and live for exemplary nature; by his injuries you have been mended.

It was Jesus' willing contribution of Himself on the Cross that bore our wrongdoings. In any case, exactly the same tortured assemblage of Jesus, in His scourging and

execution, bought for us the gift of actual mending —
"by His injuries you have been recuperated."
Furthermore, notice the distinctions in the action word
tenses utilized by Isaiah and Peter. Isaiah, prophetically
seeing this seven centuries before Christ, said, "By His
injuries we are mended." The witness Peter, thinking
back to Christ's authentic passing and revival, proclaimed,
"By His injuries you have been recuperated." Jesus
shouted out from the Cross, "It is done!" Sin has been
survived. Affliction has been survived. The Cross of
Jesus Christ has vanquished both sin and affliction. Dr.
Roger Sapp, whose Albums and DVDs on mending I
have enormously delighted in, firmly underscores that
recuperating is our own in light of what Jesus achieved at
the Cross. Jesus Christ the Hero is similarly as clearly
Jesus Christ the Healer.

CHAPTER ONE

Coming up next are a portion of the various examples of heavenly, profound mending in the Book of scriptures. How about we find out what experiences we can gain from them.

• God answers supplication for divine mending.

Beginning 20:17-18 Then Abraham appealed to God, and God recuperated Abimelech, his better half and his slave young ladies so they could have kids once more, for the Master had quit for the day belly in Abimelech's family due to Abraham's significant other Sarah.

Numbers 12:13 So Moses shouted out to the Master, "O God, if it's not too much trouble, recuperate her!"
The guideline here is straightforward — devoted Abraham implored, and God mended. Moses petitioned God for infected Miriam, and God mended her.
Ruler David figured out the force of supplication for recuperating the debilitated — "O Master my God, I

called to you for help and you recuperated me" (Hymn 30:2).

The continuous guideline seen here and somewhere else in the Book of scriptures, is the force of a devotee's request. God praises and answers petition for divine mending. Abraham, Moses, and David trusted in God's mending power and His readiness to recuperate, and they appealed to God for it. I referenced above how the Master recuperated my better half's fruitlessness. I should add that she and I and various others had been undauntedly appealing to God for recuperating of that fruitlessness. Furthermore, God was devoted to reply! Jesus showed on this equivalent force of a devotee's confidence filled petition:

Matthew 21:22 "Assuming that you accept, you will get anything you request in supplication."

• What's more, it's alright with God assuming our requests for mending are profoundly personal!

2 Lords 20:1-5 (Ruler James Rendition) In those days was Hezekiah wiped out unto demise. What's more, the prophet Isaiah the child of Amoz came to him, and said

unto him, Accordingly saith the Master, Put thine house together; for thou shalt bite the dust, and not live. Then he turned his face to the wall, and supplicated unto the Master, saying, I entreat you, O Ruler, recall now the way in which I have strolled before you in truth and with an ideal heart, and have done what is great in thy sight. Furthermore, Hezekiah sobbed sore. Furthermore, it happened, in advance of Isaiah was gone out into the center court, that the expression of the Ruler came to him, saying, Turn once more, and tell Hezekiah the commander of my kin, Hence saith the Master, the Divine force of David thy father, I have heard thy petition, I have seen thy tears: view, I will recuperate you: on the third day thou shalt go up unto the place of the Ruler.

Difficult ailments can genuinely annihilate. Ruler Hezekiah was "debilitated unto demise." To exacerbate the situation, the prophet Isaiah presented to him the Master's message that this disease would be deadly. Hezekiah's response is extremely enlightening for us.

The Holy book uncovers to us that, having discovered that his sickness was terminal, Hezekiah "sobbed harshly" (NIV) as he "supplicated unto the Master." Note that God respected both Hezekiah's request and his feelings — "I have heard thy petition; I have seen thy tears: observe, I will recuperate you." It's good with God assuming we are very personal in moving toward Him with our mending needs.

Presently we should take a gander at certain instances of Jesus recuperating the wiped out, the sick, the unhealthy, those in aggravation, and so forth.

• Jesus mended an expansive scope of ailments — truth be told, He recuperated "each illness and disorder." Matthew 4:23-24 Jesus went all through Galilee, showing in their temples, teaching the uplifting news of the realm, and Recuperating Each illness and affliction among individuals. News about him spread all over Syria, and individuals brought to him all who were sick with different illnesses, those experiencing serious agony, the devil had, those having seizures, and the incapacitated, and he mended them. (covers mine)

Christians serve a mending Friend in need, Jesus Christ. His heart, as here, is for "individuals." The Gospel records teem with representations of the recuperating wonders of Jesus among the majority, the people in the city. He taught and instructed, yes. However, He too "mended each infection and disorder among individuals." "Each infection and affliction" — Christ's mending power is unbounded. His recuperating contact is accessible to everybody. There is no disease past His capacity to fix. He mended them all, including:

• those "evil with different infections"

• the individuals who were "experiencing serious agony"

• the "devil had"

• those "having seizures"

• the individuals who were "deadened"

So make sure to any recuperating need to Jesus, on the grounds that in His service of mending, He exhibited His capacity and His readiness to recuperate "each illness and ailment among individuals."

• Jesus' recuperating power was forecasted in the Hebrew Scripture.

Matthew 8:16-17 (Ruler James Rendition) When the even was come, they brought unto him numerous that were moved by villains: and he cast out the spirits with his promise, and mended all that were debilitated: that it very well may be satisfied which was spoken by Esaias the prophet, saying, Himself took our ailments, and exposed our afflictions.

God had this as a main priority from the start. The prophet Isaiah discussed it seven centuries before the New Confirmation period:

• Jesus would take up our ailments.

• Jesus would bear our illnesses.

• Jesus would "recuperate all that were wiped out" to satisfy the prescience of Isaiah.

• Be urged to contact Jesus for your mending.

Matthew 14:35-36 (KJV) And when the men of that spot knew about [Jesus], they conveyed into all that nation indirect, and brought unto him all that were unhealthy; and besought him that they could contact the trim of his article of clothing: and as many as contacted were made totally entirety.

Refrain 36 (NIV) "...all who contacted him were mended."

Our part is to make a genuine connection with Jesus for recuperating. Carry your debilitated ones to Jesus. Urge them with an otherworldly conviction to make a genuine connection with Him, since then, at that point, as now, all who contacted Him were recuperated.

• Try not to supplicate the outcast's request; ask Jesus' response!

Mark 1:40-41 A man with uncleanliness came to him and implored him kneeling down, "In the event that you are willing, you can make me clean." Loaded up with sympathy, Jesus connected his hand and contacted the man. "I'm willing," he said. "Be spotless!"

Try not to lay out your recuperating tenet on the pariah's cry, "Assuming that you are willing." No, yet rather construct your confidence for mending on Jesus' certainty building answer, "I'm willing!" Fix this thought solidly in your spirit — Jesus Will mend the people who come to Him in confidence.

• Trust the Ruler for divine recuperating. Have Confidence an option for Him and eagerness to mend you. Matthew 9:20-22, 27-30a (KJV) And, see, a lady, which was unhealthy with an issue of blood twelve years, came behind him, and contacted the trim of his piece of clothing: For she said inside herself, In the event that I may yet contact his piece of clothing, I will be entirety. In any case, Jesus turned him about, and when he saw her, he said, Little girl, be of good solace; thy confidence hath made you entirety. What's more, the lady was restored from that hour.... [27] And when Jesus left thereupon, two visually impaired men followed him, crying, and saying, Thou Child of David, show kindness toward us. Furthermore, when he was come into the house, the visually impaired men came to him: and Jesus saith unto them, Accept ye that I am ready? They said unto him, Yea, Ruler. Then contacted he their eyes, expressing, As per your confidence be it unto you. Furthermore, their eyes were opened.

A rule critical is found in these stanzas — that is, "thy confidence hath made you entire ... as per your confidence be it unto you." Jews 11:6 lets us know that "without confidence it is difficult to satisfy God." Yet on the other hand, we are told, "In the event that you accept, you will get anything you request in supplication" (Matthew 21:22). God anticipates us, in requesting recuperating as well as in different supplications, to trust Him, to trust His statement, to "have confidence in God" (Imprint 11:22). Divine recuperating is suitably called "confidence mending"!

I recall the late Kenneth Hagin saying that he had seen numerous healing s in a non-charismatic, basic church from the get-go in his service. He said he basically taught "confidence and mending" and individuals got recuperated! He grasped that key: confidence is a basic fixing in divine mending.

• God might request that we show our confidence for profound recuperating.

Matthew 12:10, 13 And a man with a wilted hand was there. Searching for motivation to denounce Jesus, they asked him, "Is it legitimate to mend on the time of rest?" ... [13] Then he told the man, "Loosen up your hand." So he extended it and it was totally reestablished, similarly as stable as the other.

There might be times when the Ruler will request that you show your confidence, to give perceptible proof of your confidence, as on account of the man whom He told to loosen up his wilted hand. I composed before how my significant other Mickey, truly trusting God for the mending of her barrenness, felt confidence to purchase a roomful of nursery furniture. Very few months after the fact, following six years of barrenness, she found herself pregnant with the first of our four youngsters. I can presume that God saw the truthfulness of Mickey's confidence (alter 2010: see Recognition for a Day to day existence Lived Well).

• Mending comes through confidence in Jesus, not confidence in confidence.

Acts 3:16 with an otherworldly conviction for the sake of JESUS, this man whom you see and know was areas of strength for made. Jesus' name and the confidence comes through Him that has given this total recuperating to him, as may be obvious.

Mending comes "with an otherworldly conviction in" somebody — JESUS! Throughout the long term I have heard earnest Christians mislead their confidence. Some have fallen into the mistake of having "confidence in confidence." No! Our confidence is in an Individual, Jesus, who recuperates. Others have appropriately scanned the Holy book for divine recuperating Sacred texts, yet have tragically been content to utilize them simply as a "recipe" for mending, instead of as a disclosure of the Healer Himself. "Confidence recuperating" isn't basically trusting the tenet of mending (valid as that regulation is), however having faith in the Healer, the Individual — that is, in Jesus Christ.

Peter figured out the appropriate object of our confidence — Jesus! He let his audience members know how the faltering man had been recuperated:

• "...by confidence for the sake of Jesus"

• "It is Jesus' name..."

• "It is...the confidence that comes through Him..."

• At times we might have to "stroll" for some time in confidence, then, at that point, the mending comes. Luke 17:12 (KJV) And as he went into a specific town, there met him ten men that were untouchables, which stood far off: And they lifted up their voices, and said, Jesus, Expert, show kindness toward us. Furthermore, when he saw them, he said unto them, Go shew yourselves unto the ministers. Furthermore, it happened, that, as they went, they were purified.

This is an extremely consoling section. Notice that the outsiders were not recuperated the second they supplicated. No, yet rather they were recuperated "as they went" to show themselves to the ministers in acquiescence to Jesus.

There might be times as needs be "stroll" for some time in confidence, and afterward the mending comes. Albeit numerous healing s in the Book of scriptures were quick, some were not prompt. Keep up with ardent confidence as you appeal to God for divine recuperating, and cheer up in the event that your mending doesn't quickly happen.

• Try not to supplicate, then, at that point, question!

In his epistle James uncovers a significant standard for the individual requesting something from God — "When he asks, he should accept and not question, since he what doubts' identity resembles a rush of the ocean, blown and threw by the breeze. That man shouldn't figure he will get anything from the Ruler" (James 1:6-7). At the point when you ask God for mending, don't question! Try not to falter! Trust God. Trust the recuperating commitments of integrity. Reject question, picking rather to say, "God is valid ... His assertion is valid ... so my questions should go!"

• Presently how about we take a gander at how to get heavenly mending. How could it be tended to individuals?

1. By petition, as we have previously seen.

2. By an expressed word.

John 4:49-51 (KJV) The aristocrat saith unto him, Sir, descend ere my youngster kick the bucket. Jesus saith unto him, Go thy way; thy child liveth. Furthermore, the man accepted the word that Jesus had expressed unto him, and he turned out well for him. Furthermore, as he was presently going down, his workers met him, and told him, saying, Thy child liveth.

Indeed, even a good ways off from the aristocrat's home, Jesus expressed: "Thy child liveth." And the man "accepted the word that Jesus had expressed" and got back to find his child alive. There is recuperating power in the expressed expression of confidence.

Acts 9:33-34 There he found a man named Aeneas, a disabled who had been confined to bed for a very long time. "Aeneas," Peter shared with him, "Jesus Christ mends you. Get up and deal with your mat." Quickly Aeneas got up.

Once more, we see the force of the expressed expression of confidence. Peter just announced reality: "Jesus Christ recuperates you." And the supernatural occurrence of mending followed right away. Tell the wiped out, "Jesus Christ mends you." Make no expressions of remorse for that assertion. Try not to uncertainty it. Try not to attempt to dilute it. As the familiar axiom goes, more genuine words were rarely expressed!

Acts 14:8-10, KJV And there sat a specific man at Lystra, barren in his feet, being a disabled person from his mom's belly, who never had strolled: a similar heard Paul talk: who steadfastly observing him, and seeing that he had confidence to be mended, said with a boisterous voice, Stand upstanding on thy feet. Furthermore, he jumped and strolled.

Yet again we see the recuperating force of the verbally expressed expression of confidence. The proclaiming of the expression of God propelled an environment of confidence. Paul "saw that [the faltering man] had confidence to be recuperated."

How did the weak man arrive at this spot of having confidence to be mended? The response is that he heard the expression of God spoken by Paul. This is an essentially significant rule for all places of worship and all Christians. Teach the word. Show the word. God's assertion will move confidence in the listeners. Also, we will start to see emotional healing s in light of the expressed expression of confidence — "Stand upstanding on thy feet!"

3. By the laying on of hands.

Acts 9:10-11, 17-18, KJV And there was a sure devotee at Damascus, named Ananias; and to him said the Master in a dream, Ananias. What's more, he said, View, I'm here, Master. What's more, the Master said unto him, Emerge, and go into the road which is called Straight, and enquire in the place of Judas for one called Saul, of Tarsus.... [17] And Ananias turned out well for him, and went into the house; and putting his hands on him said, Sibling Saul, the Ruler, even Jesus, that seemed unto you in the way as thou camest, hath sent me, that thou mightest get thy sight, and be loaded up with the Heavenly Apparition. Furthermore, promptly there tumbled from his eyes as it had been scales: and he got sight forthwith, and emerged, and was absolved.

First notification that it doesn't need a witness to mend the wiped out. It doesn't need somebody with an extraordinary healing service to mend the wiped out.verse 10 distinguishes Ananias essentially as a "pupil." Imprint 16:17-18 records Jesus' guarantee to all devotees — "And these signs will go with the individuals who believe.... they will put their hands on debilitated individuals, and they will recover."

Driven by Jesus in a dream, the reliable follower Ananias tracked down Saul and reported to him that Jesus had sent him to mend Saul's visual deficiency. It is significant for the individuals who are debilitated to comprehend that Jesus is capable and ready to recuperate them. Then Ananias laid his hands on him, and Saul's eyes quickly got sight once more.

4. By filling the penniless individual's heart with the confidence building, nurturing expression of God.

Adages 4:20-22 My child, focus on what I say; listen near my words. Try not to let them far away from you, keep them inside your heart; for they are life to the individuals who track down them and well-being to a man's entire body.

The expressions of the Ruler, as kept in the Holy book, are nurturing. Jesus said that His words "are soul and they are life" (John 6:63). Quite possibly of the most motivating Disc I have at any point paid attention to was basically an assortment of heavenly recuperating Sacred texts read resoundingly by a minister. I could feel the expression of God building confidence.

In any case, the Maxim uncovers one more sensational advantage of keeping the Master's words "inside your heart", and that advantage is well-being — "My words ...[are] well-being to a man's entire body." The common world discusses "elective well-being". Yet, the best wellspring of elective well-being — or any part of well-being! — is the certain commitments of God in His promise, the book of scriptures.

5. Through what have been designated "petition materials."

Acts 19:11-12 God did remarkable marvels through Paul, so that even cloths and covers that had contacted him were taken to the wiped out, and their sicknesses were restored and the detestable spirits left them.

Many temples keep on imploring this way for debilitated relatives and companions who inhabit a distance. I embrace this training earnestly.

For the most part, during the post-administration special stepped area service somebody will hold a cloth over which devotees will come and petition God for mending for the individual out of luck. Then the tissue is sent to the wiped out individual, alongside some confidence building sacred texts on divine recuperating (as a rule including Acts 19:11-12) and a clarification that professors in the congregation had petitioned God for them for their mending. Declarations proliferate of individuals being truly mended along these lines.

Quite a long time back in a congregation in Dock, I was contacted to see a clinical specialist holding a request fabric for the benefit of a wiped out individual of his colleague. As I got together with the others in petition, I contemplated internally, "Here is this Christian specialist, with all his logical information, unassumingly requesting that the Incomparable Doctor show improvement over clinical science can make it happen." My confidence was supported.

6. A joyful heart adds to our getting profound mending. Maxims 17:22 A lively heart is great medication, yet a squashed soul evaporates the bones.

(Ruler James Rendition) A joyful heart doeth great like a medication: however a messed up soul drieth the bones. The edge of the New American Standard Book of scriptures says that an upbeat heart "in a real sense, 'causes great mending.' "

Consider that — the condition of our "heart" — alluding here to the feelings, not the real organ — can significantly influence our great well being or scarcity in that department. This has for quite some time been widely known in the clinical field. Once in a while diseases are analyzed as "psychosomatic" in beginning. Curiously, the word psychosomatic comes from the very Greek words that the Book of scriptures utilizes for "soul" and "body." So clinical science concurs with the Holy book that the condition of our internal man or lady can considerably influence our actual well being, for good or for terrible.

The expression of God says that a happy heart "in a real sense causes great recuperating"! There is an immediate, circumstances and logical results result: happy heart — great recuperating. On the other hand, a wrecked or squashed soul adversely affects our well-being (it "evaporates the bones").

One of the products of the Soul (Galatians 5:22) is euphoria. The people who permit the presence of the Ruler in their lives to bring a day to day, internal bliss will likewise procure the brilliant commitment of their "cheerful heart doing great like a medication."

7. There is recuperating in "the Ruler's Dinner," the Fellowship.

1 Corinthians 11:29-30 For anybody who eats and beverages [the Ruler's dinner, versus 20] without perceiving the body of the Master eats and beverages judgment on himself. For that reason numerous among you are frail and debilitated, and various you have nodded off.

"That is the reason many...are frail and wiped out." Why? They take Communion "without perceiving the body of the Master." They fail to remember 1 Peter 2:24 — "By his injuries you have been mended." They partake in the fellowship administration, maybe requiring an actual recuperating, and stay careless in regards to the way that Jesus' body bore both our wrongdoings and our disorders. I would urge each per-user to contemplate these things the following time you take communion. Recollect how Jesus' messed up body has helped you. Get the advantages of that leaning on an unshakable conviction. Furthermore, anticipate that mending should come to your body, in any event, during the very fellowship administration.

8. By calling the seniors of the congregation to lay on hands, bless with oil, and petition God for you.

James 5:14-15 Is any of you debilitated? He ought to call the seniors of the congregation to ask over him and bless him with oil for the sake of the Ruler. Also, the request presented in confidence will make the wiped out individual well; the Master will raise him up.

A significant doctrinal point on a connected subject — each congregation should have elderly folks. In any case, there are no "elderly folks of the congregation" for the wiped out to call for petition and blessing with oil. Might you at any point distinguish the elderly folks of your congregation?

In my years as a Christian, I have been a senior in three neighborhood houses of worship. I have consistently thought of it as an honor to answer calls from the wiped out. The cycle is basic and will for the most part be something like this:

1. The wiped out individual, or somebody for their sake, calls a senior to come and implore.

2. That senior contacts one more senior or two to go with him.

3. Those elderly folks bless the debilitated individual with oil and ask the "request of confidence" (KJV).

4. That being finished, God's commitment is: "The Master will raise him up."

9. In certain occasions, divine mending comes as evil presences are driven out. [NOTE: The Good book doesn't show that devils can possess Christians.]

Matthew 17:15, 18 "Master, show kindness toward my child," he said. "He has seizures and is enduring significantly. He frequently falls into the fire or into the water." ... [18] Jesus reprimanded the devil, and it emerged from the kid, and he was mended from that second.

It is critical to advise ourselves that this recuperating was before the Cross of Christ, so the kid was not a brought back to life individual, inhabited by the Essence of God. I find no Book of scriptures proof that a brought back to life Christian can be moved by an evil spirit.

Here the kid was plainly moved by had an evil presence inside (refrain 18 — "it emerged"). The devil's presence was appeared by the kid having seizures. At the point when Jesus cast out the devil, the kid was quickly recuperated.

You also may experience a few cases of torments endured by unsaved individuals that are brought about by devilish power. As on account of Jesus restoring the epileptic kid, mending might come as you drive the demon(s) away for the sake of the Ruler Jesus Christ.

Luke 13:10-13 On a Sabbath Jesus was showing in one of the temples, and a lady was there who had been disabled by a soul for a very long time. She was twisted around and couldn't fix up by any means. At the point when Jesus saw her, he called her forward and shared with her, "Lady, you are liberated from your sickness." Then, at that point, he put his hands on her, and quickly she fixed up and adulated God.

This is a comparable occurrence to the recuperating of the epileptic kid. The lady had been in a real sense "disabled by a soul" for a long time. Jesus recognized (refrain 16) that Satan had bound her and that she should have been "set free." He served that redemption to her, and she was quickly mended from her devastating condition.

10. At times mending comes from what might appear to us to be fairly strange, even surprising, strategies.

John 9:6-7 Having said this, he spit on the ground, made some mud with the salivation, and put it on the [blind] man's eyes. "Go," he told him, "wash in the Pool of

Siloam" (this word implies Sent). So the man proceeded to wash, and got back home seeing.

Acts 5:15-16, KJV Since that they carried forward the debilitated into the roads, and laid them on beds and love seats, that essentially the shadow of Peter passing by could eclipse some of them. There came likewise a huge number out of the urban communities indirect unto Jerusalem, bringing debilitated people, and them which were vexed with messy spirits: and they were mended each one.

Jesus spit, made mud, and put it on a visually impaired man's eyes. Also, when the man washed his eyes, he could see! Debilitated individuals were laid in the roads, and when Peter's shadow disregarded them, they were mended.

These and other phenomenal healing s were not composed to give us a "design" of how to clergyman to the debilitated. Truth be told, neither of these cases was rehashed in the New Confirmation. These are essentially indications of the complex force of God to recuperate. As we have found in things 1-10 above, God recuperates in different ways. The shared factor in everything is this: God mends!

WHO might be accustomed to get mending to those need?

1. Eventually, otherworldly recuperating in all examples continues from God.

2. The early missionaries recuperated.

Matthew 10:1, 8 He called his twelve pupils to him and gave them position to drive out detestable spirits and to mend each infection and sickness.... [8] Mend the debilitated, raise the dead, scrub the people who have sickness, drive out evil presences. Uninhibitedly you have gotten, openly give.

Acts 3:6-7 Then [the apostle] Peter said, "Silver or gold I don't have, yet what I have I give you. For the sake of Jesus Christ of Nazareth, walk." Taking him by the right hand, he helped him up, and in a flash the man's feet and lower legs became solid.

3. A bigger gathering of 72 followers was sent by Jesus to mend the debilitated.

Luke 10:1, 8-9 After this the Ruler named 72 others and sent them in pairs in front of him to each town and spot where he was going to go.... [8] "When you enter a town and are invited, eat what is set before you. Mend the wiped out who are there and tell them, 'The realm of God is close to you.'

4. In the Incomparable Commission, Jesus urged all devotees to mend the debilitated.

Mark 16:15-18, KJV And he said unto them, Go ye into all the world, and teach the gospel to each animal. He that believeth and is absolved will be saved; however he that believeth not will be cursed. Also, these signs will follow them that accept; In my name will they cast out demons; they will talk with new tongues; They will take up snakes; and assuming they drink any lethal thing, it will not hurt them; they will lay hands on the wiped out, and they will recuperate.

The Incomparable Commission is for all devotees to share the Uplifting news of Jesus "in all the world." And God will affirm the Gospel with extraordinary signs, including healing s. What's more, the Gospel that He will affirm isn't spoken just by witnesses and other appointed priests, yet in addition by "them that accept" (17). Each adherent can share the Uplifting news and can serve divine recuperating today to the debilitated. Jesus' consolation to each adherent is (18): "Lay hands on the sick, also, they will recuperate."

5. There are a few Christians (not all) who are particularly engaged by the Essence of God with "gifts of mending."

1 Corinthians 12:7-11, KJV Yet the indication of the Soul is given to each man to benefit withal. For to one is provided by the Soul with the useful tidbit; to one more the expression of information by a similar Soul; to one more confidence by a similar Soul; to one more the gifts of recuperating by a similar Soul; to one more the working of marvels; to another prediction; to another insightful of spirits; to one more jumpers sorts of tongues; to one more the translation of tongues: Yet every one of these worketh that one and the equivalent Soul, partitioning to each man severally as he will.

This rundown is normally called the nine profound gifts or gifts of the Essence of God. These are heavenly gifts with which the Essence of God supplies individual Christians to priest to other people.

One of these nine is "gifts of recuperating." It is given to some, not all — notice: "to one is given ... to another ... to another ... to one more the gifts of recuperating ..."

1 Corinthians 12:28-30a And in the congregation God has named most importantly missionaries, second prophets, third educators, then, at that point, laborers of marvels, likewise those having gifts of recuperating, those ready to help other people, those with gifts of organization, and those talking in various types of tongues. Are missionaries? Are prophets? Are instructors? Do all work wonders? Do all have gifts of recuperating? This is a comparable rundown of otherworldly gifts and services, demonstrating that to some God disperses the particular "gifts of recuperating."

Allow me to add a side idea before our outline. It is this: Confidence doesn't block our utilizing astuteness and taking typical disinfectant, antibacterial precautionary measures. For instance:

2 Rulers 20:7 Then Isaiah [the prophet] said, "Set up a poultice of figs." They did so and applied it to the bubble, and he recuperated.

Luke 10:34 "He went to him and dressed his injuries, pouring on oil and wine." [The wine, containing liquor, would have an antibacterial effect.]

1 Timothy 5:23 "Quit drinking just water, and utilize a little wine as a result of your stomach and your continuous diseases." [Apparently, in setting, for the liquor's disinfectant properties when filled debased water. It appears to be that microbe loaded water was giving Timothy repeating stomach problems.]

The superb English Book of scriptures educator Smith Wigglesworth used to tell about voyaging one day in a rail route mentor. Two others on the train — a mother and little girl — were extremely wiped out, so Wigglesworth told them, "Look, I've something taken care of that will fix each case on the planet. It has never been known to fizzle."

The mother and little girl were very intrigued, so the priest proceeded to enlighten them concerning this "cure." When they at long last requested a portion, he opened the pack, took out his Book of scriptures, and read the stanza that says, "I'm the Master who healeth you" (Departure 15:26, KJV).

What a great method for sharing how the Book of scriptures is loaded up with commitments and records in regards to well-being and recuperating for His youngsters. God is and has forever been the Healer!

Mending All through the Book of scriptures

God's always present longing for us is reflected in His Departure 15:26 contract with the offspring of Israel. David recognizes that agreement as he composes:

Favor the Master, O my spirit, and all that is inside me, favor his sacred name! Favor the Ruler, O my spirit, and fail to remember not every one of his advantages, who excuses generally your wrongdoing, who recuperates every one of your sicknesses. (Song 103:1-3, ESV)

Moreover, the New Confirmation records how Jesus helped the wiped out, doing supernatural occurrences and mending all who came to Him:

What's more, he went all through all Galilee, showing in their places of worship and broadcasting the good news of the realm and mending each sickness and each difficulty among individuals. (Matthew 4:23)

Mending is all through the Holy book. As a matter of fact, not long before Jesus climbed into paradise, He talked distinctly to His devotees of the signs that would go with adherents, including "they will lay their hands on the wiped out, and they will recuperate" (Imprint 16:18).

The blessing was areas of strength for so the messengers that astonishing supernatural occurrences followed any place they served:

Presently many signs and ponders were routinely finished among individuals by the hands of the witnesses. Furthermore, they were all together in Solomon's Patio. None of the rest thought for even a moment to go along with them, however individuals held them in high regard. Also, like never before adherents were added to the

Master, huge numbers of all kinds of people, so they even did the debilitated into the roads and laid them on beds and mats, that as Peter dropped by basically his shadow could fall on some of them. Individuals likewise accumulated from the towns around Jerusalem, carrying the wiped out and those beset with messy spirits, and they were totally mended. (Acts 5:12-16)

Upon God's Promise, let me guarantee you that today: God's will is for you to stroll in divine recuperating and well-being!

CHAPTER TWO

However, there is something else to find about marvel mending — a great deal more!

Explanations behind Recuperating

In the beginning of our service, I started to see individuals mended who had next to no confidence. I asked exclusive who came to the stage to affirm about his marvel, "What church do you join in?"

"I don't go to chapel," he answered.

"Are you a Christian?" I addressed.

"No, sir," he said obtusely. "I know nothing about that." Here was an individual who had no information on the Word, had never given his heart to Christ, yet was currently recuperated. I shared with myself, "Ruler, this doesn't appear to be legit!"

Before long, I had a discussion with Dr. Lester Sumrall, an extraordinary man of confidence who has since proceeded to brilliance. I inquired, "Could you at any point clear up for me why God is recuperating such countless unbelievers in our gatherings?"

He answered with this inquiry: "Who did Jesus recuperate quite a while back?"

I returned to my Book of scriptures and checked on the supernatural occurrences of Christ and the messengers. A large number of times, our Master Jesus and His supporters served mending even to those with practically no comprehension of the things of God.

I started to understand that His leniency brings both salvation and the supernatural.

Also, mending is accessible to you at this moment!

Seven Purposes for Divine Recuperating Today

Whenever I return to my review notes from that time in my life after my discussion with Dr. Sumrall, it is in every case such a joy to go through what the Ruler showed me.

I've been helped to remember those words and the section commonly lately, and I need to share seven of God's many purposes or explanations behind mending individuals — then and presently.

Reason 1: Jesus mends since He is brimming with sympathy.

An outcast came to Jesus "entreating him, and bowing shared with him, 'Maybe, you can make me clean'" (Imprint 1:40).

What was the Ruler's reaction? Moved with feel sorry for, he loosened up his hand and contacted him and told him, "I will; be spotless." And quickly the sickness left him, and he was made clean. (Mark 1:41-42)

It was empathy that prompted the marvel. Jesus Christ mends individuals today for a similar explanation: "Or do you impose upon the wealth of his thoughtfulness and restraint and persistence, not realizing that God's consideration is intended to lead you to contrition?" (Romans 2:4).

Reason 2: Jesus mends since recuperating has a place with His youngsters.

Once, when Jesus was teaching close to the city of Tire, a Syrophenician fell at His feet, requesting that he cast a messy soul out of her little girl.

Jesus shared with her, "'Let the kids be taken care of first, for it isn't all in all correct to take the youngsters' bread and toss it to the canines.' However she responded to him,

'Indeed, Ruler; yet even the canines under the table eat the youngsters' scraps'" (Imprint 7:27-28).

The Master saw the lady's confidence, and the little girl was conveyed!

Assuming you are an offspring of the Ruler, it could appear to be that mending ought to come to you first, even before unbelievers get wonders. However I watch as the individuals who don't have the foggiest idea about the Ruler connect in extraordinary confidence, hungry for the "morsels," and a large number of times He spills out His mending excellence upon these individuals.

Say thanks to God, recuperating is much of the time the section point that assists individuals with getting Jesus Christ as Hero!

Reason 3: Jesus mends to carry brilliance to His Dad.

On a mountain close to the ocean of Galilee, we are told: Incredible groups came to him, carrying with them the weak, the visually impaired, the injured, the quiet, and numerous others, and they put them at his feet, and he mended them, so the group pondered, when they saw the quiet talking, the disabled sound, the faltering strolling, and the visually impaired seeing. Furthermore, they celebrated the Lord of Israel. (Matthew 15:30-31)

On another event, there was a comparative reaction when Jesus recuperated an immobile man, and "When the groups saw it, they were apprehensive, and they celebrated God, who had given such power to men" (Matthew 9:8).

Maybe the group didn't comprehend that the "man" with such extraordinary authority was the Child of God, yet they were moved enough by what they saw to extol God. Recuperating is a great, sensational confidence manufacturer that ought to prompt extolling Him.

Reason 4: Jesus mends to satisfy God's commitments.

At Capernaum one night, "They brought to him numerous who were mistreated by devils, and he cast out the spirits with a word and recuperated all who were debilitated. This was to satisfy what was spoken by the prophet Isaiah: 'He took our ailments and bore our illnesses'" (Matthew 8:16-17).

At the point when the Expert mends, it is a satisfaction of the prediction expressed through Isaiah and the Hebrew

Scripture. On the cross, Christ took our ailment and illnesses.

Reason 5: Jesus recuperates likewise to affirm His own Assertion.

Mending was guaranteed by the Dad, then, at that point, proclaimed by Jesus Christ. He said:

In the event that I am not doing crafted by my Dad, then don't trust me; however assuming I do them, despite the fact that you don't really accept that me, accept the works, that you might be aware and comprehend that the Dad is in me and I'm in the Dad. (John 10:37-38)

Christ knew precisely why He was shipped off earth. He came to play out crafted by His Dad. Supernatural occurrences affirm the expressed expression of Jesus. He mends to satisfy His own statement to you.

Reason 6: Jesus recuperates to show you the power in His blood.

The prescience announced in Isaiah 54:4-5 was satisfied 20 centuries prior:

Most likely he has borne our distresses and conveyed our distresses; yet we regarded him stricken, stricken by God, and burdened. In any case, he was penetrated for our offenses; he was squashed for our evildoing s; upon him was the rebuke that brought us harmony, and with his injuries we are mended.

The blood of Jesus was shed to excuse sin and give recuperating — then, at that point, and presently!

Reason 7: Each time the Ruler recuperates, Satan's loss at the cross is uncovered indeed.

The Word tells us, "The explanation the Child of God seemed was to annihilate crafted by Satan" (1 John 3:8).

At the place of Cornelius, the witness Peter said:

You yourselves realize what occurred all through all Judea, starting from Galilee after the sanctification that John declared: how God blessed Jesus of Nazareth with the Essence of God and with power. He approached accomplishing something useful and mending all who were abused by Satan, for God was with him. (Acts 10:37-38)

We have the victory! We can live in win step by step!

Jesus has a deep understanding of you. He needs awesome for you. You are His fortune. He even knows the quantity of hairs on your head (Matthew 10:29-31). He wants to have pity and mending toward you. You are valuable to the point that He passed on the cross for your wrongdoing and your ailments. Allow the Incomparable Doctor to carry recuperating and redemption to you today! God maintains that you should live in divine recuperating and well-being. He believes you should see increasingly more about divine mending.

That is my request for you — an existence of supernatural occurrence mending and well-being — today and consistently!

Co-Workers for the Reason for Christ

The world is biting the dust to catch wind of this bountiful existence of marvels!

The call of mankind has gotten stronger, yet the sob for the Gospel is the most intense ever, and I'm more dedicated today than any time in recent memory to broadcast the groundbreaking and marvel working message of Christ!

This is really a thrilling hour for this service.

Will you assist me with telling the lost through our day to day This Is Your Day communicates, Supernatural occurrence Recuperating Administrations, the Web, virtual entertainment, and each of our efforts through each mean conceivable?

Will you assist me educate them concerning our Master Jesus Christ with viability and power, that Jesus and just Jesus is the Savior?

How about we make our valuable Jesus pleased as we look to satisfy the Incomparable Commission together! God is opening fantastic entryways, and I maintain that you should be essential for this prophetic open door. I'm requesting that you give today toward what God is doing in our middle. Anything that God puts on your heart to do, kindly submit to Him!

He wants to favor you so you can a favor. Furthermore, what a gift you are as you plant into the ripe fields of this global service as we travel through our 46th year!

I'm asking you, in all sincerity, to give liberally today for this strong work of God so we can keep on taking the

Uplifting news of Jesus Christ through the marvelous, remarkable entryways He is opening to us.

Salvation, recuperating, and supernatural occurrences are more essential today than any other time in recent memory, and we can assist with satisfying the Incomparable Commission during the next few days.

I'm anticipating hearing from you! Not exclusively will your seed go toward the proclaiming of the Gospel to the countries from one side of the planet to the other, however you will plant toward an extraordinary reap in your own life.

For the superb and everlasting reason for our valuable Master Jesus Christ.